How to do Fractions

by

Ian Wallace Campbell

COPYRIGHT

This electronic version first published in 2013

by Ian Wallace Campbell

ISBN-13:
978-1492846420

ISBN-10:
1492846422

Liability Disclaimer

By reading this book, you assume all risks associated with using the advice given below, with a full understanding that you, solely, are responsible for anything that may occur as a result of putting this information into action in any way, and regardless of your interpretation of the advice.

You further agree that our company cannot be held responsible in any way for the success or failure of your business as a result of the information presented in this book. It is your responsibility to conduct your own due diligence regarding the safe and successful operation of your business if you intend to apply any of our information in any way to your business operations.

Terms of Use

About the author

Ian Wallace Campbell is a photographer, journalist, author, writer and a teacher of mathematics. He holds a B.Sc. degree in Physics and a Post Graduate Certificate in Education (Math) and has more than ten years experience in teaching the subject.

Contents

Introduction

Is math difficult for you to understand? Do you hate it as a subject because it is too difficult to do? Is it really too difficult for you or are you just frightened of it because you don't understand its language? If the answer to any of these questions is 'yes' then I can probably help you.

This book is to enable you to handle fractions. Fractions are one of many topics that you have to be able to handle in order to get your grade in mathematics. A lot of people hate things that they don't, won't or can't understand but my purpose in this book is to teach you how to handle fractions. It starts by explaining what fractions are (as if you didn't know) and then takes you step by step through the process of adding fractions together; taking one fraction from another; multiplying two fractions together and lastly dividing one fraction by another.

If you are wide awake when you start this book, then I reckon I can teach you all about fractions in very little time. All you have to do is pay attention and work through the examples in the book. The system works because it teaches you in an unusual way which I call the 'Magic Arrow Method'. The arrows in question are used to show you the order in which a series of simple calculations must be made. These calculations are simple multiplications and if you know your tables, then they are really very easy. I wish I could claim the method as my own invention, but I can't. What I can tell you, is that in all my experience as a math teacher, this is the easiest way I know of teaching fractions and I wish I had learnt the method when I was at school; it would have saved me heaps of time!

The way to use this book is simple. The method for each manipulation is very similar in all cases. Just study the examples and follow along with pen and paper. Check the answers on a calculator if you wish, just to convince yourself that the method really does work.

Good luck!

FRACTIONS

Let's think of a bar of chocolate. We unwrap the bar and see that the chocolate bar is divided into squares of chocolate which we can break off. Let's say that our bar of chocolate has eight segments arranged in two rows of four segments. It's a small bar of chocolate but I want to keep things simple for the moment so that you can see and understand the fractions I am going to give you so that you can convince yourself that the breaking up of the bar of chocolate gives you the same answer as the mathematical explanation.

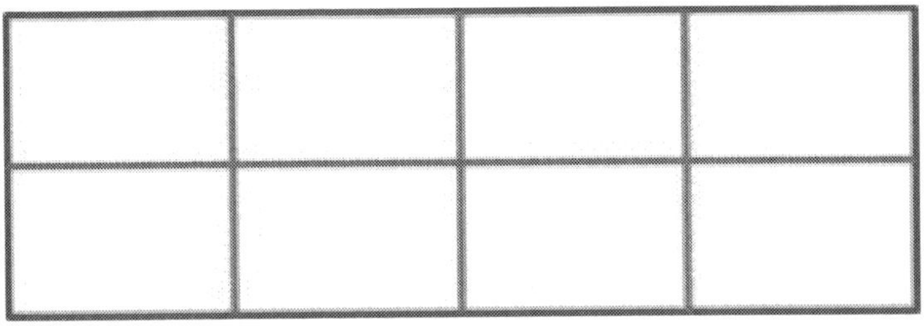

This is the whole bar of chocolate which has 8 pieces. We are going to add together two different sized fractions of this bar of chocolate. One half of the bar (4 pieces) plus one quarter of the bar, (2 pieces). The question is 'what fraction of the bar do we have if we add the half bar and quarter bar together?

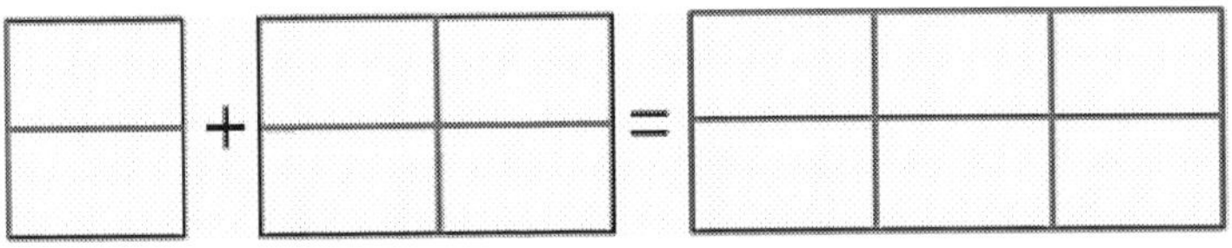

If we add the pieces together we can see that we have 4 pieces in the half-bar plus 2 pieces in the quarter bar giving us 6 pieces altogether. If the whole bar had 8 pieces and we now have only 6 pieces, then we have 6/8 or ¾ of the whole bar.

The Old-fashioned Method

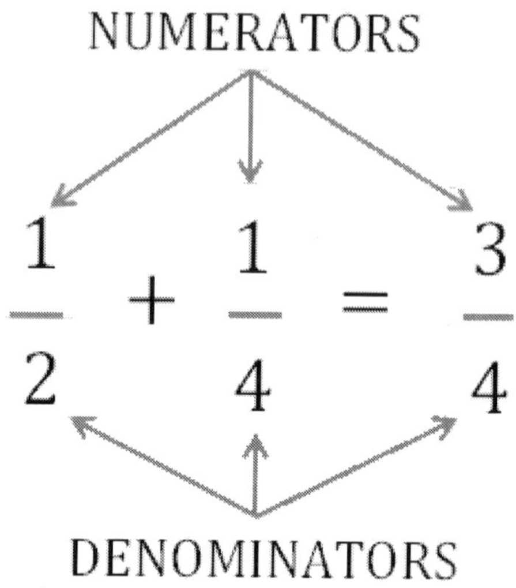

You can see that the word ‘numerator’ is the name for the parts of the fractions above the line. ‘Denominator’ is the correct name for the parts of the fraction below the line. We would then be told that as the denominators in the two fractions were different, that we would have to find a common denominator before we could solve the problem. The denominator of ½ is 2 and the denominator of ¼ is 4. Which number divides an exact number of times into 2 and 4? Here the answer is simple as both the 4 and the 2 divide into 4. This means that we can re-write the fraction over a common denominator and the new numerator value(s) accordingly.

$$\frac{2}{4} + \frac{1}{4} = \frac{3}{4}$$

Confused? You won’t be !

The Magic Arrow System

Using this system, we can solve any fraction problem simply.

The way we do this is to use 'arrows' to help us remember the order in which to perform the simple steps necessary to solving fraction problems.

For addition and subtraction the arrows are numbered:-

1 ⟶

2 ⟶

3 ⟶

and we follow the numbered arrow sequence from 1 to 3.

For multiplication and division, there are only two arrows which appear in the following directions:-

Left to right across the tops and bottoms of the fractions.

Bearing these simple instructions in mind, in order to add, subtract, multiply and divide fractions we simply have to follow the numbered arrows in sequence and perform simple multiplications of the numbers and to take note of the sign involved.

Let's start with the addition of two simple fractions. Addition and subtraction are the most difficult of the four functions because we have to express the numerators (the tops of the fractions) in terms of a common denominator (the bottoms of the fractions). Fortunately this is easy to do with the Magic Arrow method.

$$\frac{1}{2} + \frac{1}{4} = \frac{3}{4}$$

We are going to start with this nice, simple fraction. The first thing to do is to draw our 'Magic Arrows' over the top of it so that we can see from them the order in which we should do everything.

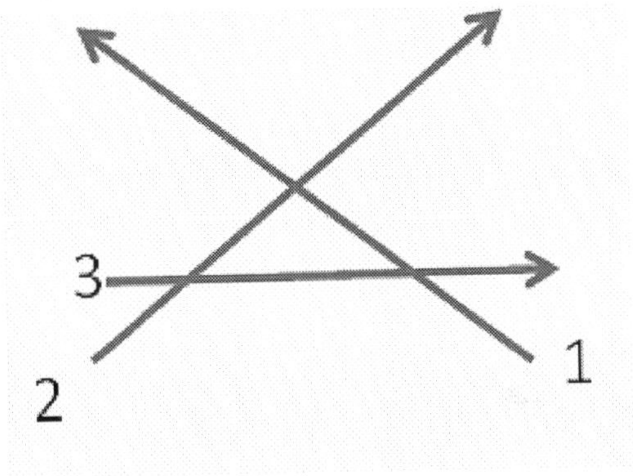

For fraction problems of addition or subtraction, the arrows always run in these directions; bottom right to top left is always the first thing to do and we shall call it Arrow 1. Then the second thing to do is Arrow 2 which runs from the bottom left to the top right and finally the last thing is to place Arrow 3 from left to right.

You should now have something that looks like this, with the three arrows superimposed over the fraction.

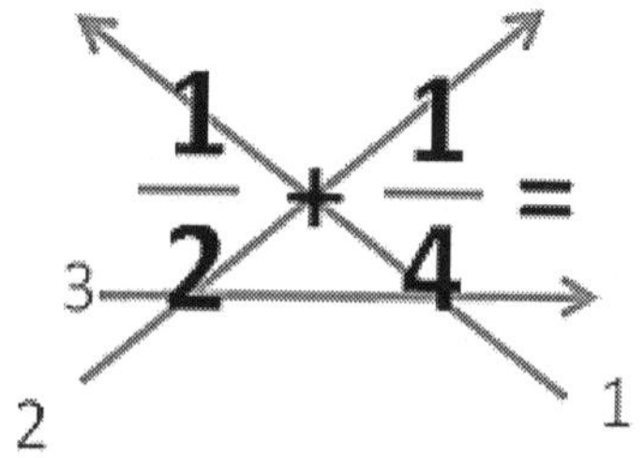

That's the hard part done! Now find Arrow 1 and notice that it runs through the number 4 at the bottom right, to number 1 at the top left. Multiply these together.

4 x 1 = 4

Write this value in at the tip of Arrow 1 and do the same for Arrows 2 and 3.

Arrow 2 is 2 x 1 = 2

Arrow 3 is 2 x 4 = 8

Write these values respectively at the tips of arrows 2 and 3.

With luck your working out should look like the picture below:-

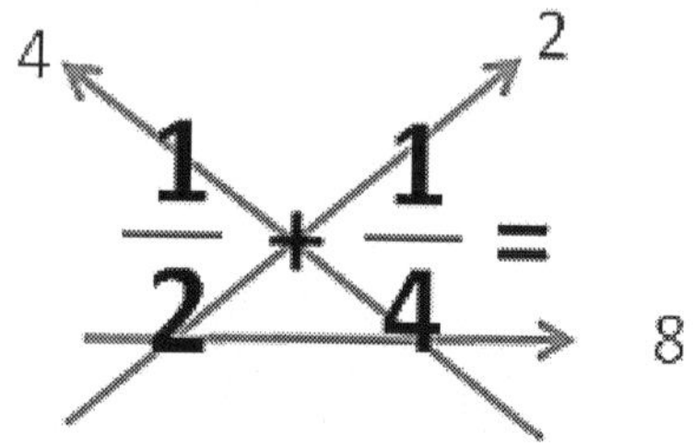

This calculation enables us to re-write the equation using the new Numerator and Denominator values.

$$\frac{4}{8} + \frac{2}{8} = \frac{6}{8}$$

Which gives us the answer of six-eighths (6/8), but we can see that we can cancel this down by dividing the top and bottom of the fraction by 2 which gives the answer three-quarters (3/4).

$$\frac{\overset{3}{\cancel{6}}}{\underset{4}{\cancel{8}}} = \frac{3}{4}$$

Cancelling down

$$\frac{\overset{3}{\cancel{6}}}{\underset{4}{\cancel{8}}} = \frac{3}{4}$$

Look at the problem above. Ask yourself 'how many twos are there in six?" The answer is 'three'. So cross out the six and write in 'three'. Now look at the bottom of the fraction… '8'. 'How many twos are there in eight?' The answer is 'four' so cross out the 'eight' and write in 'four'. Because we can divide the top and bottom of the fraction by the same whole number, exactly, without a remainder we can re-write the fraction 6/8 as ¾. This process is called 'simplification' or 'simplifying fractions' or 'cancelling down'.

Think back to the chocolate bar explanation of what a fraction was. If our chocolate bar consisted of eight squares of chocolate then you can see that half the bar would have four pieces and that a quarter of the bar would have had two pieces. If you add them together then you have 4 + 2 which is 6 pieces of chocolate out of a total of 8 pieces. This is written as 6/8 or ¾.

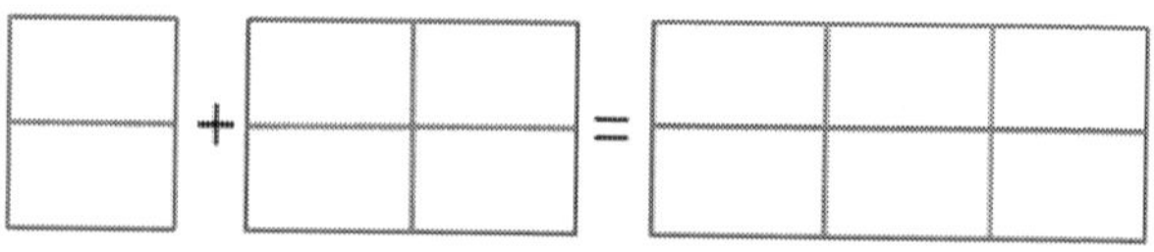

Subtracting fractions

Subtracting fractions is as easy as adding them together. We use three arrows in the same directions. The only difference is in the sign. Let's look at an example using the same fractions as we have just used in the addition example.

$$\frac{1}{2} - \frac{1}{4} =$$

We start in the same way as with the addition problem by drawing the arrows over the equation.

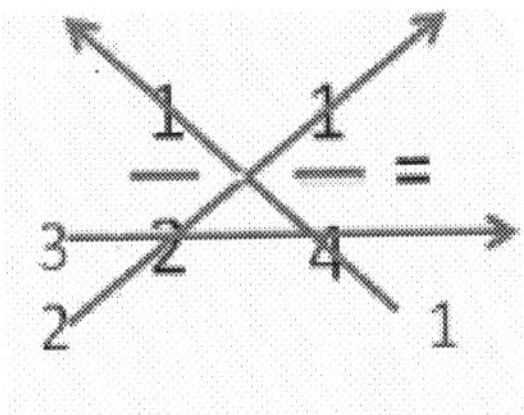

Calculate the numbers to write in at the tips of the arrows. This should give you the fractions like this:-

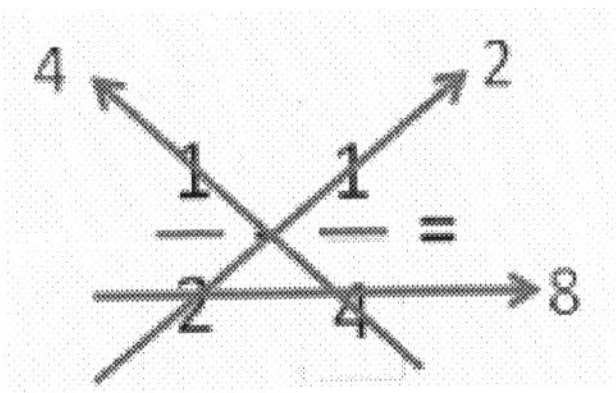

Re-write the problem using the new numerator and denominator values you have calculated in the last step. You should have something like this:-

$$\frac{4}{8} - \frac{2}{8} = \frac{2}{8}$$

This can be simplified by dividing the top and bottom of the fraction by 2 to give the answer of one quarter.

$$\frac{\overset{1}{\cancel{2}}}{\underset{4}{\cancel{8}}} = \frac{1}{4}$$

Multiplication of fractions

The multiplication and division of fractions is much easier than the addition and subtraction of them because there are fewer steps and things are more straight-forward. They only involve two arrows instead of three!

We will use the same fractions again in this example.

$$\frac{1}{2} \times \frac{1}{4} = \frac{1}{8}$$

Now add the arrows. There are only two and they go straight across the tops of the fractions and the bottoms of the fractions.

$$\frac{1}{2} \times \frac{4}{1} \rightarrow = \frac{4}{2}$$

The first of next two examples can be simplified but the second, can't be simplified:-

$$\frac{3}{8} \times \frac{4}{5} =$$

$$\frac{3}{8} \times \frac{4}{5} \rightarrow = \frac{12}{40}$$

$$\frac{\overset{3}{\cancel{12}}}{\underset{10}{\cancel{40}}} = \frac{3}{10}$$

Sometimes the result cannot be simplified as in the example below.

$$\frac{9}{17} \times \frac{3}{5} = \frac{27}{85}$$

Division

Let's start with something simple so that you can see what the answer should be. Then we will apply the Magic Arrows to see how they work. It is easy to see that there are three quarters in the fraction ¾. So let's use this easy example for which we already know the answer to see how the Magic Arrow method works with division.

The problem is simply the division of one fraction by another. There are some rules for doing this. Change the sign to its opposite and turn the second fraction upside-down. Then treat it as a multiplication problem and multiply the numbers using the arrows. Finally, simplify the answer by dividing top and bottom by 4.

Our task here is a simple one; to divide one simple fraction by another.

$$\frac{3}{4} \div \frac{1}{4} =$$

Before we can do this, we have to remember the method or 'trick' for doing so which is to change the sign to its opposite sign and turn the second fraction upside down. if we do this we can treat the problem as a multiplication which is a lot simpler to do!

$$\frac{3}{4} \times \frac{4}{1} = \frac{12}{4}$$

By re-writing the problem this way, we merely have to multiply the tops and the bottoms.

$$\frac{\overset{3}{\cancel{12}}}{\underset{1}{\cancel{4}}} = 3$$

Simplify the answer by cancelling down, and dividing top and bottom by 4.

Even when the fractions involved are nastier, the method is still the same.

Consider the following fractions:-

$$\frac{9}{17} \div \frac{3}{5} =$$

These are truly horrible fractions because their denominators are so different and you will not find a common denominator for them that is smaller than 51 (17 x 3). Just remember the method. Change the division sign to its opposite and turn the second fraction upside down.

$$\frac{9}{17} \times \frac{5}{3} = \frac{45}{51}$$

Multiply the numerators (tops) and multiply the denominators (bottoms).

$$\frac{\overset{15}{\cancel{45}}}{\underset{17}{\cancel{51}}} = \frac{15}{17}$$

The answer is 45/51 which can be cancelled down by dividing both top and bottom by 3. So this turned out to be a lot easier than it looked and was easily solved by applying the 'Magic Arrows' method!

The method is very similar to multiplying two fractions together but involves one extra step… turning the second fraction upside-down and changing the sign from ÷ to x.

After a while you can dispense with the arrows. So that's it. You now know how to add, subtract, multiply and divide fractions and it wasn't that difficult!

Now for some practice. Write out the following problems; draw in the Magic Arrows and solve them.

Exercise 1

1.	$\frac{4}{8} - \frac{3}{8} =$	11.	$11 \times \frac{1}{2} =$
2.	$\frac{5}{13} + \frac{1}{2} =$	12.	$4 \times \frac{3}{4} =$
3.	$\frac{1}{2} + \frac{1}{4} =$	13.	$\frac{1}{2} \times \frac{1}{4} =$
4.	$\frac{7}{8} + \frac{4}{8} =$	14.	$10 \times \frac{2}{5} =$
5.	$\frac{7}{10} + \frac{1}{4} =$	15.	$1 \div \frac{1}{8} =$
6.	$\frac{7}{10} - \frac{1}{4} =$	16.	$1 \div \frac{1}{5} =$
7.	$\frac{4}{8} + \frac{3}{8} =$	17.	$\frac{3}{4} \div 4 =$
8.	$\frac{1}{3} - \frac{1}{7} =$	18.	$\frac{4}{5} \div 5 =$
9.	$\frac{7}{8} \div 3 =$	19.	$\frac{5}{8} \div \frac{1}{4} =$
10.	$\frac{9}{16} \div \frac{4}{5} =$	20.	$\frac{2}{3} + \frac{1}{5} =$

Mixed Fractions

From time to time you will meet a mixed fraction which looks like this:-

$$1\frac{1}{8} + 2\frac{5}{8} =$$

Before you can manipulate it you have to convert it to a 'top-heavy' or 'improper' fraction.

Look at the denominator… this is how many parts the whole number is divided into. So, in this example 'one and one eighth', the 'one' can be represented as 'eight eighths' or 8/8. Additionally we have one eighth as well, (1/8). As 1/8 plus 8/8 add together to give 9/8 we can see that we write 'one and one-eighth' as 'nine-eighths'.

Suppose we are asked to add 'one and one-eighth' to 'two and five-eighths'. We have to convert both fractions to 'improper' fractions before we begin. We can write 'two and five-eighths' as 'twenty-one eighths', (2 X 8 = 16, plus 5 gives 21 eighths)

The problem then is:-

$$1\frac{1}{8} + 2\frac{5}{8} \rightarrow \frac{9}{8} + \frac{21}{8} = \frac{30}{8} \rightarrow 3\frac{6}{8} = 3\frac{3}{4}$$

Convert the Mixed Numbers to 'top-heavy' fractions over the common denominator, '8'.

This changes 1 and 1/8 to 9/8 and 2 and 5/8 to 21/8.

As the Denominators are the same we can just add the tops together and write them over the common denominator, 8.

So 9/8 plus 21/8 = 30/8… a 'top-heavy' fraction.

Divide the 'top' (30) by the 'bottom (8) which gives three and a remainder of six-eighths. Recognise that this can be cancelled down by dividing 'top' and 'bottom' by 2 which leaves the answer three and three quarters (3 and ¾).

This was a simple example of adding fractions. It was simple because both fractions were in terms of eighths. In other words, they had the same denominator but what if they had had different denominators? Consider the following problem:-

$$3\frac{4}{7} + 2\frac{3}{5} =$$

We are asked to add together two mixed number fractions. First we have to convert them into 'top heavy' fractions and then use the arrows and work out the values.

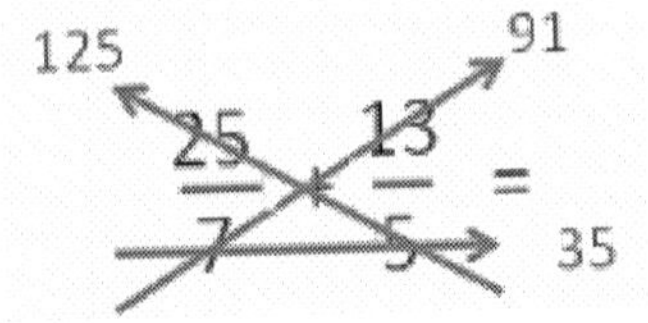

Re-write using the new numerators and the common denominator.

$$\frac{125}{35} + \frac{91}{35} = \frac{216}{35}$$

Add the tops up and write this over the Common Denominator.

$$\frac{216}{35} = 6\frac{6}{35}$$

Divide the top by the bottom to give you the new mixed number fraction.

Of course, it is just as easy to subtract, multiply and divide mixed number fractions as you will see in the following examples.

$$3\frac{4}{7} - 2\frac{3}{5} =$$

This is very similar to the previous problem except that we are subtracting the smaller fraction from the larger one instead of adding the two fractions together. Because of this, the only real difference is in the sign.

Re-write as 'top heavy' fractions, use the arrows and calculate the new numerators and the common denominator.

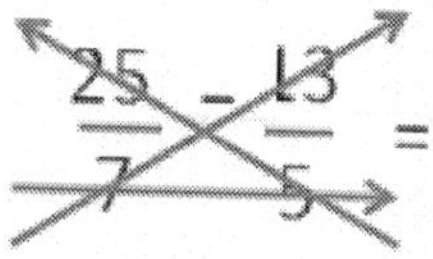

This should give you the values shown below.

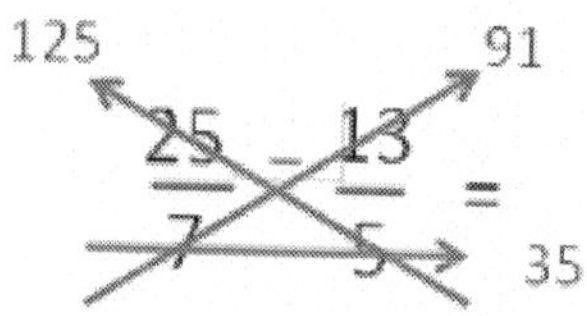

Calculate the numerators in terms of 35ths.

$$\frac{125}{35} - \frac{91}{35} = \frac{34}{35}$$

Multiplication (mixed number fractions)

Consider the following fractions:-

$$3\frac{4}{7} \times 2\frac{3}{5}$$

The first step in solving this is to change the mixed number fractions into a 'top-heavy' fractions. Multiply the tops and multiply the bottoms.

$$\frac{25}{7} \times \frac{13}{5} = \frac{325}{35}$$

Notice that the top and bottom can each be divided by 5 to give you 65/7 which is an easier fraction to simplify because the numbers are smaller.

$$\frac{65}{7} \rightarrow 9\frac{2}{7}$$

Likewise, the division of mixed number fractions is just as easy, except that it contains just one more step.

$$3\frac{4}{7} \div 2\frac{3}{5}$$

First we have to convert these mixed number fractions into 'top-heavy' ones.

$$\frac{25}{7} \div \frac{13}{5} =$$

Now it is more manageable, the next step is to change the sign to its opposite and to turn the second fraction upside-down; then use the arrows.

$$\frac{25}{7} \times \frac{5}{13} = \frac{125}{91}$$

Multiply the tops and the bottoms.

$$\frac{125}{91} = 1\frac{34}{91}$$

And finally, divide the top by the bottom.

Answers

1.	$\frac{4}{8} - \frac{3}{8} = \frac{1}{8}$	As the Denominators are the same, just subtract the Numerators from each other and place the result over the common Denominator.
2.	$\frac{5}{13} + \frac{1}{2} = \frac{23}{26}$	Use the Magic Arrow method.
3.	$\frac{1}{2} + \frac{1}{4} = \frac{3}{4}$	Use the Magic Arrow method.
4.	$\frac{7}{8} + \frac{4}{8} = \frac{11}{8} = 1\frac{3}{8}$	As the Denominators are the same, just add the Numerators together over the common Denominator to get the 'top-heavy' fraction, then simplify by dividing the Numerator by the Denominator.
5.	$\frac{7}{10} + \frac{1}{4} = \frac{38}{40} = \frac{19}{20}$	Use the Magic Arrow method to get 19/20 then simplify by dividing Numerator and Denominator by '2'.

6.	$\frac{7}{10} - \frac{1}{4} = \frac{18}{40} = \frac{9}{20}$	Use the Magic Arrows & simplify the answer.
7.	$\frac{4}{8} + \frac{3}{8} = \frac{7}{8}$	Because the Denominators are the same, just add the Numerators together.
8.	$\frac{1}{3} - \frac{1}{7} = \frac{4}{21}$	Use the Magic Arrow method.
9.	$\frac{7}{8} \div 3 \rightarrow \frac{7}{8} \times \frac{1}{3} = \frac{7}{24}$	Write the '3' as 3/1 as this 'balances' the fractions. Then change the sign to its opposite sign and turn the second fraction 'upside-down'. Multiply the tops and then the bottoms.
10.	$\frac{9}{16} \div \frac{4}{5} \rightarrow \frac{9}{16} \times \frac{5}{4} = \frac{45}{64}$	Change the sign to 'X'; turn the second fraction 'upside-down'; multiply the tops and the bottoms.

11.	$\frac{11}{1} \times \frac{1}{2} = \frac{11}{2} = 5\frac{1}{2}$	Multiply the tops; multiply the bottoms; simplify.
12.	$\frac{4}{1} \times \frac{3}{4} = \frac{12}{4} = 3$	Multiply the tops; multiply the bottoms; simplify.
13.	$\frac{1}{2} \times \frac{1}{4} = \frac{1}{8}$	Multiply the tops; multiply the bottoms; simplify.
14.	$\frac{10}{1} \times \frac{2}{5} = \frac{20}{5} = 4$	Multiply the tops; multiply the bottoms; simplify.
15.	$1 \div \frac{1}{8} \rightarrow \frac{1}{1} \times \frac{8}{1} = 8$	Re-write; change the sign & turn the second fraction upside down; multiply the tops & multiply the bottoms.

16.	$1 \div \frac{1}{5} \rightarrow \frac{1}{1} \times \frac{5}{1} = 5$	Change sign; invert 2nd fraction; multiply tops & bottoms.
17.	$\frac{3}{4} \div \frac{4}{1} \rightarrow \frac{3}{4} \times \frac{1}{4} = \frac{3}{16}$	Change sign; invert 2nd fraction; multiply tops & bottoms..
18.	$\frac{4}{5} \div \frac{5}{1} \rightarrow \frac{4}{5} \times \frac{1}{5} = \frac{4}{25}$	Change sign; invert 2nd fraction; multiply tops & bottoms.
19.	$\frac{5}{8} \div \frac{1}{4} \rightarrow \frac{5}{8} \times \frac{4}{1} = \frac{20}{8} = 2\frac{1}{2}$	Change sign; invert 2nd fraction; multiply tops & bottoms; divide top by bottom.
20.	$\frac{2}{3} \div \frac{1}{5} \rightarrow \frac{2}{3} \times \frac{5}{1} = \frac{10}{3} = 3\frac{1}{3}$	Change sign; invert 2nd fraction; multiply tops & bottoms; divide top by bottom.

Glossary

Adding fractions ... is simple, if the denominators are the same. Otherwise, we have to find the Lowest Common Denominator by using the Magic Arrows method.	$\frac{5}{13}+\frac{1}{2}=\frac{23}{26}$
Cancelling down or simplifying a fraction. Sometimes the outcome of the manipulation of a fraction results in an answer like 24/32. This fraction may be simplified by cancelling down. In this case, divide top and bottom by 8 to give ¾. Fractions should always be simplified wherever possible and extra marks are often awarded for this in an exam.	$\frac{\overset{3}{\not{24}}}{\underset{4}{\not{32}}}$
Common Denominator When the value of the bottom parts of both fractions are the same.	$\frac{4}{8}+\frac{2}{8}=\frac{6}{8}$
Denominator The bottom part of the fraction.	

Division of fractions by whole numbers. The 'trick' here is to write the whole number as a fraction. In this case we write 4 as 4/1 which makes it easier to apply the Magic Arrows method.	$\frac{1}{3} \div 4 \rightarrow \frac{1}{3} \times \frac{1}{4} = \frac{1}{12}$
Division of fractions by fractions. Change the sign for its opposite (÷ becomes X); invert the 2nd fraction then use the multiplication method.	$\frac{1}{3} \div \frac{1}{4} \rightarrow \frac{1}{3} \times \frac{4}{1} = \frac{4}{3} = 1\frac{1}{3}$
A Mixed Fraction consists of a whole number and a fraction. Before you begin you need to change everything into the same units. Here, if the fraction is in thirds, then express the mixed fraction as thirds. How many thirds are there in '2', answer '6'. So we have 6/3 plus 1/3 (from the fraction part) which gives us 7/3 in all.	$2\frac{1}{3}$
Multiplication of fractions. This is the easiest to do. The Magic Arrow method has one arrow passing through the Numerators and another passing through the Denominators. Simply multiply the tops together and then multiply the bottoms together.	$\frac{2}{3} \times \frac{4}{5} = \frac{8}{15}$

Numerator	The ‘top’ part of the fraction.
Subtracting fractions Subtracting one fraction from another is very simple if both fractions have a common denominator.	$\frac{4}{8} - \frac{2}{8} = \frac{2}{8}$
However, if the denominators are different it is not so simple. This is where we use the ‘Magic Arrows’ to find out what the new numerators will be in terms of a common denominator.	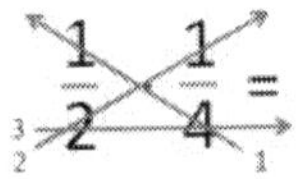 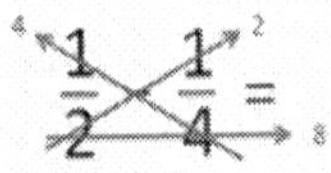 $\frac{1}{2} - \frac{1}{4} = \frac{2}{8} = \frac{1}{4}$
Top-heavy fractions A ‘Top-heavy’ fraction or ‘Improper’ fraction is one where the numerator (top) has a larger value than the denominator (bottom).	$\frac{4}{3} = 1\frac{1}{3}$

The End

Other books by the author

One man's revenge against the banks. Pascoe is ruined by his wife and left with a mountain of debt which he can't pay. Faced with bankruptcy he decides to use his skills to get his rveenge on the system by creating his own bank!

Paperback

ISBN-10: 1453713700

ISBN-13: 978-1453713709

Kindle ASIN: B004183MXE

The sequel to *That Will Do Nicey*. Pascoe and Sam have built and opened a holiday centre for artists in the spectacular countryside around Rennes-le-Château, France. They have just finished their first season when a horrific murder happens on their doorstep!

Paperback

ISBN-10: 1453755527

ISBN-13: 978-1453755525 Kindle ASIN: B00DT5HHDQ

A collection of short stories by the author when he was learning about great French wines in the Haut Médoc region of France between 1979 and 1986. If you love wine, you'll love these informative and entertaing tales.

Vendange, Kindle ASIN: B006H3K72A

The author's collaboration with David Wood into the mysteries associated with Rennes-le-Château, France. *Geneset - Target Earth* tells of the warning etched into 40 square miles of the French countryside and is the real story behind the DaVinci Code.

Geneset Dossiers: Paperback

ISBN-10: 1453713700

ISBN-13: 978-1453713709 Kindle ASIN: B004183MXE

The great French painter, Nicholas Poussin and his part in the great mystery of Rennes-le-Château. This booklet explains how the geometry that underlies the painting *les Bergers d'Arcadie* is based on the same geometry discovered in the landscape.

Paperback:

ISBN-10: 1873335245

ISBN-13: 978-1873335246

Printed in Dunstable, United Kingdom

70790327R00025